COUNTING BLESSINGS

DEBBY BOONE

Illustrated by
Gabriel Ferrer

Harvest House Publishers
Eugene, Oregon 97402

HB ET

COUNTING BLESSINGS

Copyright ©1998 by Resi, Inc.
Published by Harvest House Publishers
Eugene, Oregon 97402

Library of Congress Cataloging-in-Publication Data

Boone, Debby.
    Counting blessings / Debby Boone; illustrations by Gabriel Ferrer.
        p. cm.
    Summary: Simple text and illustrations describe how thinking about
all the blessings in one's life leads to happiness and to being a
blessing to others.
    Summary: ll 1b06 03-11-98 NO illus.
    ISBN 0-7369-0026-8
    1. Happiness—Juvenile literature.   2. Happiness—Religious
aspects—Juvenile literature. [1. Happiness—Religious aspects.]
I. Ferrer, Gabriel, illu. II Title.
BJ1481.B66   1998
179'. 9—dc21   98-14872
                                                        CIP
                                                         AC

Design by Koechel Peterson & Associates, Minneapolis, Minnesota

Printed in the United States of America.

98 99 00 01 02 03 04 05 06 07 / W2 / 10 9 8 7 6 5 4 3 2 1

SECRET OF HAPPINESS.

DO YOU WANT ME
TO TELL YOU?

YOU KNOW, THINGS THAT YOU
ARE THANKFUL FOR...
THINGS THAT YOU ARE
HAPPY ABOUT...

DID YOU EVER TRY NOT TO
LAUGH WHEN
SOMEBODY WAS TICKLING YOU?

WELL, WHEN YOU
COUNT YOUR BLESSINGS,
IT'S LIKE GETTING
TICKLED ON THE INSIDE.

YOUR FROWN TURNS UPSIDE DOWN,

AND YOUR HEART
BEGINS TO SING!!!

COME ON! LET'S TRY IT!
RIGHT HERE! RIGHT NOW!

LET'S START WITH THREE.
I'LL GO FIRST.

#1 my EYES...

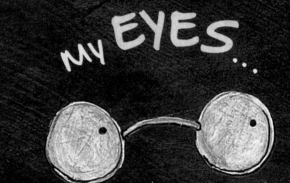

SO I CAN SEE ALL THE
BLESSINGS AROUND ME.
LIKE...

#2

MY FAT **CAT** CLEO.

ASLEEP ON MY BED.
WHICH IS ACTUALLY,

#3

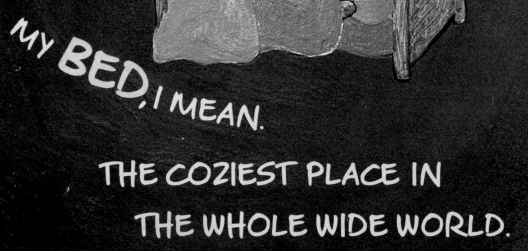

MY **BED**, I MEAN.

THE COZIEST PLACE IN
THE WHOLE WIDE WORLD.

NOW IT'S YOUR TURN!

COUNT YOUR BLESSINGS—
ONE, TWO, THREE.

BY YOURSELF, OR HERE WITH ME.
COUNT THE BLESSINGS IN PLAIN VIEW,

OR CLOSE YOUR EYES AND SEE A FEW.
COUNT THEM STANDING ON YOUR HEAD,
COUNT THEM WHILE YOU LIE IN BED.
KEEP A FEW IN YOUR BACK POCKET,
TUCK A FEW INSIDE A LOCKET.
COUNT YOUR BLESSINGS WHEN
  YOU'RE BLUE.
COUNT THEM WHEN YOU'RE HAPPY, TOO.

WHEN I FIRST STARTED,
I WROTE A FEW BLESSINGS
DOWN EACH DAY AND
KEPT THEM IN A BOX.

TWO WEEKS LATER,
I READ THEM ALL AT ONCE.
WOW! DID I FEEL HAPPY!
NOW I CAN'T STOP.

I'M COUNTING BLESSINGS INSIDE.

I'M COUNTING BLESSINGS OUTSIDE.

BLESSINGS

THAT

START

WITH THE

LETTER "P"

(OR ANY

OTHER LETTER),

BLESSINGS
THAT GO
FROM A TO Z
(A PERSONAL
FAVORITE).
A
Z
HOW MANY BLESSINGS CAN I COUNT
IN A MINUTE?

BLESSINGS THAT RHYME.

(THIS TAKES AN EXPERT!)

THANK YOU FOR
THE BIG GREEN TREE

WITH THE TREE HOUSE
THAT DAD MADE
FOR ME.

FOR ALL THE TOYS AND
ALL THE FUN

MY FRIENDS AND I HAVE
IN THE SUN.

THERE
ARE NO
RULES.

NO BLESSING IS TOO BIG

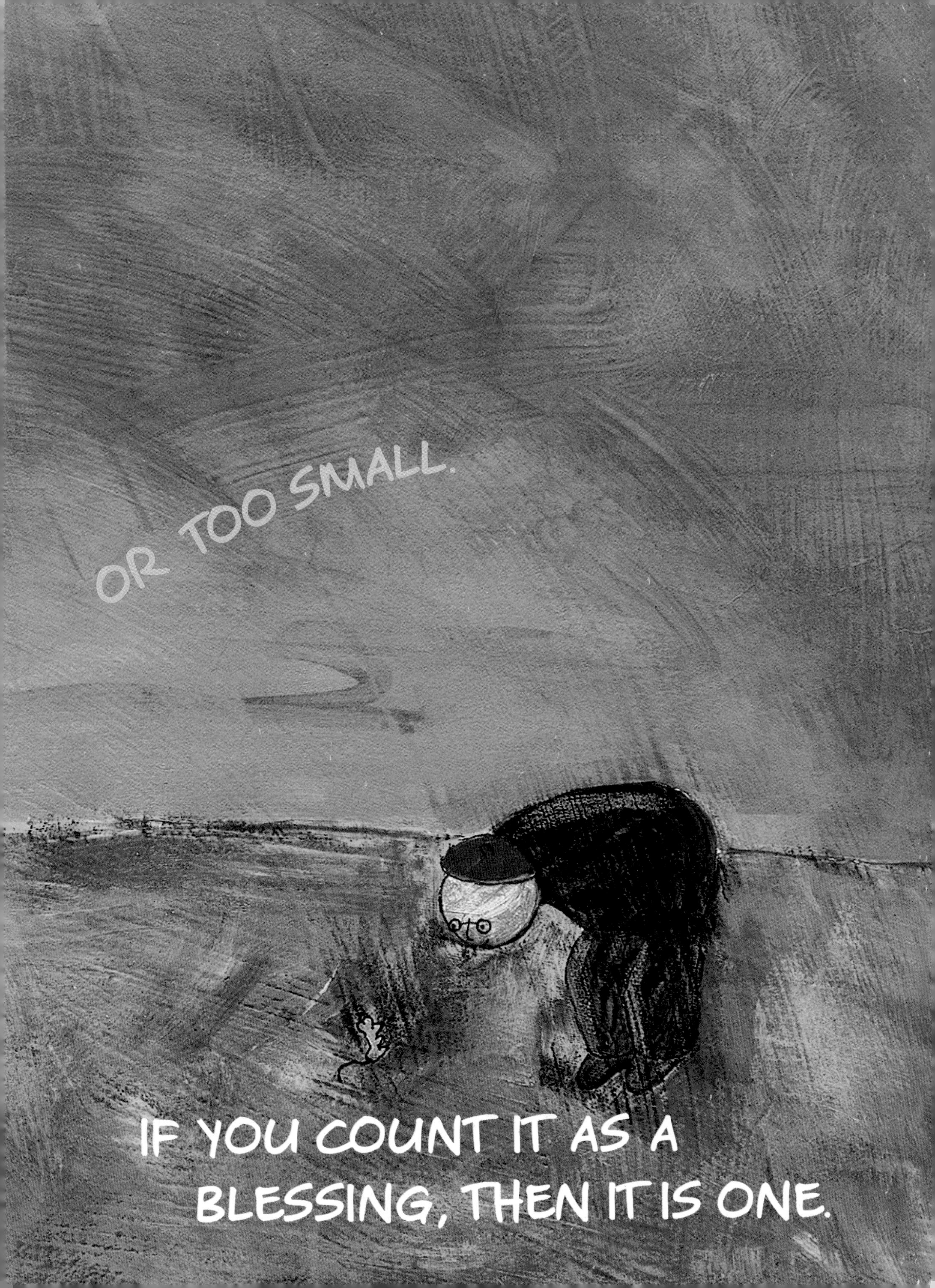
OR TOO SMALL.
IF YOU COUNT IT AS A BLESSING, THEN IT IS ONE.

HERE'S THE DEAL.

THINK ABOUT THINGS

THAT MAKE YOU SAD, YOU'LL BE SAD

THINK ABOUT THINGS IN YOUR LIFE THAT MAKE YOU HAPPY,

YOU'LL BE HAPPY.

TAKE IT FROM ME,

ONCE YOU REALIZE HOW
FULL OF BLESSINGS YOUR
LIFE REALLY IS,

YOU'LL FEEL ALMOST LIKE
YOU'RE GOING TO EXPLODE.
AND THAT'S GREAT!

BECAUSE THAT'S WHEN YOU
START LOOKING AROUND
FOR WAYS TO BECOME A
BLESSING TO SOMEONE ELSE.

A SMILE.

A KIND WORD.

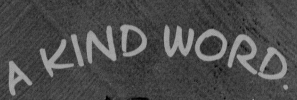

BON JOUR!

A HELPING HAND.

A HUG.

BLESSINGS ARE LIKE HUGS

FROM GOD TO LET YOU

KNOW HOW MUCH

HE LOVES YOU.